Shining Brass

THE STORY OF THE TRUMPET
AND OTHER BRASS INSTRUMENTS

By DANIEL B. TETZLAFF

Illustrated by GEORGE OVERLIE

Prepared under the supervision of Robert W. Surplus

Musical Books for Young People

LERNER PUBLICATIONS COMPANY
MINNEAPOLIS, MINNESOTA

J
788.1
T

CONTENTS

Shining Brass

The shining brass instruments of the band and orchestra interest everyone. We hear them every day on radio and television, in the movies, and on home hi-fi records. We see them playing together at concerts and in parades. Brass instruments are found in almost all musical organizations — bands, orchestras, and dance bands.

The instrument which attracts the most attention is the trumpet. It looks easy to play, since it has only three buttons to push. In any neighborhood you can usually find several boys and girls who play the trumpet. It must be fun. We see trumpets everywhere in music, don't we—in the school band, at the circus, at parades, and at park concerts.

The trumpet is one of the most important instruments in any band or orchestra. It can be played up high—almost where our voices sing the melody of a song. It can play even much higher than most peoples' voices can go. It can be played very loudly or very softly. It can be tongued very sharply or played very smoothly. No matter how it is played, all trumpet players must play very carefully. They take their responsibilities very seriously, because everyone can easily hear the parts they play.

Yes, trumpets are very important to modern orchestras and bands. They are also needed in even the smallest of groups which we call *combos*. Sometimes combos have only four or five instruments in them, instead of ten or twenty.

Musicians say that the violin is the "Queen of the string instruments". If you know about her, you know a lot about her whole family. Although different in size, the strings are all very much alike. We can also say that the trumpet is the "King of the brasses". When you learn all about the King, you will know and like all of his close relatives, too.

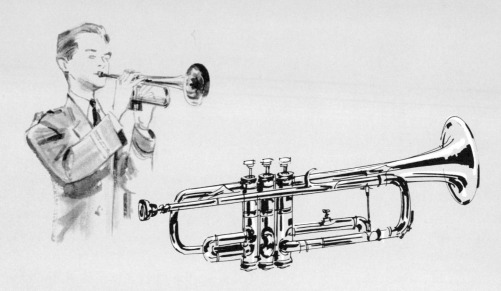

The Trumpet

In starting to learn about the trumpet, let's pretend there are no valves. There have been trumpets for about 2,000 years. They were once like what we today call a *bugle*. Fathers can't get along without bugles at veterans reunions, and sons need them at Boy Scout meetings and campouts.

Now there is no law against using the imagination, so let's pretend to uncoil the tube and straighten it out like this.

We would not have a new idea, for trumpets were made like this way back in Bible times. We see them like this in movies about the famous armies of the Romans. We can sometimes see a modern version of a straight trumpet at a college football game, since many bands use these *herald trumpets* for special fanfares. Herald trumpets are long and heavy. Also, the bell is so far away from the player that he cannot hear what he is playing. These are two good reasons why the long tube is coiled up as we see it today.

7

A long, straight brass trumpet tube is very much like an organ pipe. If we think a moment, we remember that high notes come out of little thin pipes, and low notes come out of big, thick, long ones. This is so for trumpets as well as other members of the shining brass family.

Actually, trumpets are made in several different lengths. Today, the most commonly used trumpet is the trumpet in B♭.

It is about 54 inches long. It takes a tube that long to sound the note B♭ shown here.

It is nine notes lower than middle C, and is usually written in the bass or *F-clef.*

If we cut off about six inches of the B♭ tube and made it only 48 inches long, the trumpet would sound one step higher in the scale. In other words, it would go up from B♭ to C.

The length of the tube is one thing that makes the notes higher or lower. But what makes the sound, or the music? The air inside the pipe must be made to move back and forth very, very fast, or to *vibrate.* It does this about 500 times a second when the trumpet plays its tuning note.

On the violin, the string is the vibrator. It is the *friction,* or rubbing of the bow across a string, that starts the sound. With the clarinet, you blow your breath across a little piece of wood called the *reed.* The wood of the reed vibrates, and so does the air behind it in the long black tube. In the pipe organ, a motor blows air across a little strip of metal which the organ pipe uses as a reed. The harmonica and accordion also use metal reeds.

8

Brass players must make their lips act as reeds. When they blow their breath across them, the air in a shining brass tube vibrates like the air in an organ pipe, or like the string on the violin.

Let's learn more about the bugle before talking more about the trumpet. Many boys want to learn at least the three most useful bugle calls within the first few weeks that they play. Have you heard the calls shown below? Can you remember how they go? Could you sing them? Use the words to help. Notice how the notes jump up and down, and do not step along the scale.

Did you notice that all the way through the three bugle calls, only four notes were used? Remembering the names of the lines and spaces in the treble or *G clef,* the notes used, from bottom to top are G, C, E, G.

Sol Do Mi Sol

The bugler blows the different notes by making the muscles in the center of his lips tighten or loosen, like you can with a rubber band. We will learn more about that later. Can the bugle make more than four notes? Yes. It can make ten, or even more, but the middle four are the easiest. Lower notes are a little bit hard to loosen up for, and the higher notes take time and practice to make the lip muscles strong enough.

Can you imagine what a thrill it must be for a boy to learn to play this next famous call for the first time? We hear it so often on radio and television. Actually, it is a famous piece of music called "The Overture to William Tell". You know the story: A father has to shoot an apple from his son's head.

INTRODUCTION TO THE FINALE OF "WILLIAM TELL"

Modern bugles are not pitched in C, the key with no sharps or flats. To make the notes easier to play, the bugle is in the key of G, which is four notes lower. This means that the tube is long enough to sound the first note you see on the grand staff.

10

Music has very many connections with science and mathematics. People who like to know what makes things work will want to know about this. The air waves inside the brass tubes vibrate in different ways for each of the different notes. For the lowest note, which we call the *fundamental,* the air vibrates from end to end, like this.

Did you ever shake the rope when playing jump rope? The faster you shake it, the more bumps you can make in it. It is the same with air waves in the tube. When they occur twice as fast, the note that sounds jumps up eight steps of the scale, or as we say in music, *an octave higher.* So the waves for the second note would look like this.

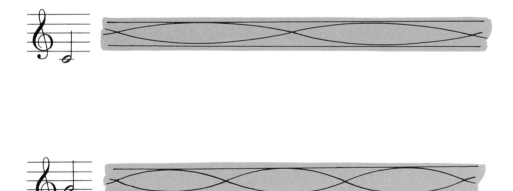

Three times faster looks like this.

How To Do It Yourself

Wouldn't you like to try to make these notes yourself? Most people can if they really want to.

To play any of the shining brass instruments, the sound is started by the player's lips.

The lips are set into vibration, like your vocal chords are, by the air from your lungs passing through them. The lungs are like "a big gas tank", and the breath in them is "the fuel".

Here is how to form the lips:

1. Hook a little rim of the red flesh of your upper lip over the teeth to hide the edge. Use a little more of the lower lip to cover the lower teeth.

2. Close your lips gently together. Now feel one lip against the other lip. Next, pretend to hold a toothpick between your lips.

3. Then hide a little bit of the lower lip under the upper. Keep the lips gently closed. Place two fingers one-half inch apart against the lips to help steady them, and to "shorten them across".

4. Next you take a big, big breath. It is all right to breathe in through both the mouth and nose. Just be sure to do the same thing the man at the gas station does when dad drives in and says, "Fill 'er up!" Or, remember what you do before you get ready to swim under water.

5. While holding the lips steady and closed and stretched a bit over the edges of the teeth, let some breath seep out through the center of the mouth. It is like what would happen if we pulled out the imaginary toothpick we were holding.

6. Keep the breath flowing out like you would to make it crawl along a sixteen-foot-long ribbon. At first just try to keep the lip muscles holding around the air hole, like the spokes of a wheel hold the hub strong and firm. This keeps the lips making the same note for a long time, which is the first thing to learn in order to play a shining brass instrument.

Many people can do this on the very first try. No one should blow hard, or force, or get red in the face. It is not necessary to struggle if you follow the directions. Just imitate what happens when you blow up a toy balloon, stretch its lips till they touch together, and then let the air out through them to make it "squeal".

The next step is to learn how to make the lip muscles a little bit tighter, or looser, so the sound will go up or down a step of the scale or two. In other words, the lip muscles follow the same little ups and downs in the scale that a melody makes, tightening for high notes and loosening for the lower notes.

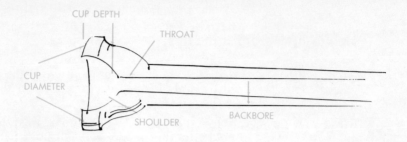

CUP DEPTH

THROAT

CUP
DIAMETER

SHOULDER

BACKBORE

Now let's get acquainted with the mouthpiece, because it is about the most important part of the instrument. It is like the carburetor of dad's car. All the fuel (breath) from the tank (lungs) must pass through this important control point.

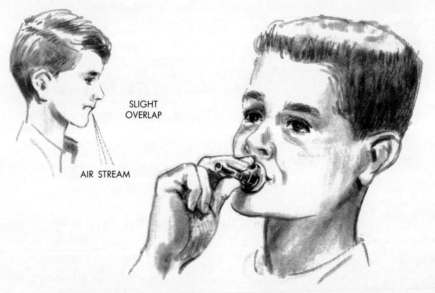

SLIGHT
OVERLAP

AIR STREAM

1. The rim of the mouthpiece acts as a kind of gentle clamp to help hold the lips together so they vibrate more easily.

2. The cup holds the vibrating center part of the lip muscles and sets up vibrating air—which sounds the same as the lips do—but quite a bit louder.

3. Cups that are wide help produce low notes.

4. Cups that are deep help produce a smooth tone.

14

Remember, the way high notes and low notes are made on cup-mouthpiece instruments is by changing the *tension,* or tightness, of the lip muscles in the center of the mouth. It is a good idea to practice with the mouthpiece alone.

Remember to fill the lungs full. Try for a "high note", but do not struggle. Make it sound for as long as you can. Then try it again to make sure.

To make a "low note", relax the lips a little, but not too much! Guess at the distance between the two notes, and then make another that will fit right in the middle.

After trying it several times, the top and bottom notes should be an octave (eight notes) apart. With the in-between note, it should look like this, and sound like what is written here.

With a little practice, you can learn to play the mouthpiece alone. Start with the top note first. Then very slowly and carefully let the lips loosen as little as possible. The tone will slide down the scale, like it does when you pull the ring out on a slide whistle.

More practice teaches the lips how to stop at any step of the scale. A bugle cannot do this, but a valve trumpet can.

It took a long time for someone to figure out a reliable and easy way to fix up a bugle or a plain trumpet with valves, so it could play all the notes of the scales like the other instruments.

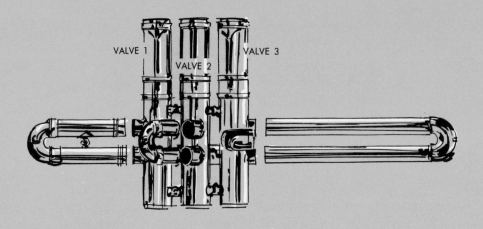

VALVE 1   VALVE 3

VALVE 2

About Valves

The important thing to remember about valves is that they make notes go lower. A shining brass instrument without valves can only play "bugle call notes", (do-mi-sol) as the breath goes straight through the tube.

However, when a valve is pressed down, the air has to make a detour and take a longer way around to get out the bell. This is a way of making the tube longer. We remember that longer pipes make lower notes.

If you will look carefully, you will see that the tube coming out of the middle valve is the shortest (on the trumpet it is about three inches long). The one coming out of the first valve is twice as long. The one on the third valve is three times as long as the second.

In music, this means that the middle valve, when pressed down, lowers any open (bugle call) note a half-step in the scale. On the piano this is like going from a white key to the nearest black one below.

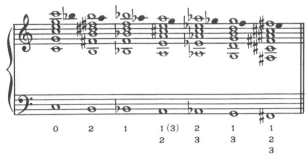

The first valve makes a note go down a whole step. A whole step is the same as two half-steps.

More than one valve at a time can be used, so the detours can be made longer and longer and in different combinations. Altogether, there are seven different combinations. Don't you admire the man who was clever enough to figure it all out for us? The man's name was Blühmel. His country was Germany, and the year was 1815.

Trumpets with valves can play any melody. Any tune you can hum, sing, or whistle, can be played. All the regular scales, and the scale with all the sharps and flats (the *chromatic scale)* are made easy with valves.

DIATONIC SCALE

CHROMATIC
SCALE

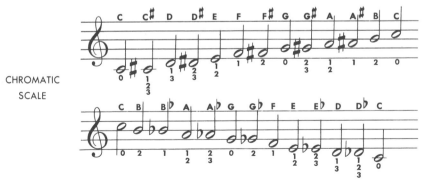

17

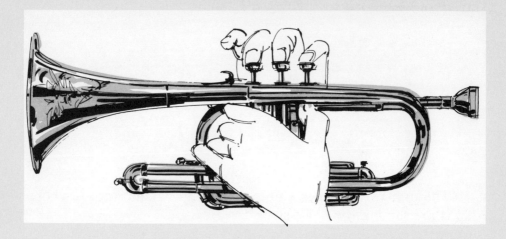

Could you hum these scales, especially if someone guided you on the piano? Read the note names out loud. Press down the fingers the directions call for on imaginary valves while you hum. Go slowly. Imagine you are actually playing the scales.

Taken all apart, a trumpet has about 200 separate pieces. Put back together again, these are the main parts to remember.

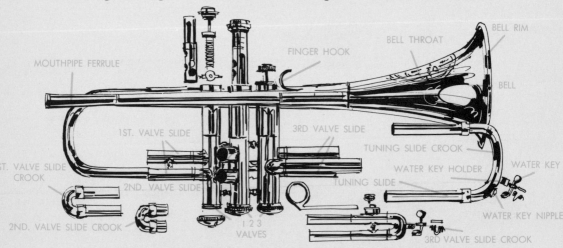

All of the members of the shining brass family have many, many parts in common. After you learn about one instrument, it is fun to figure out the others for yourself.

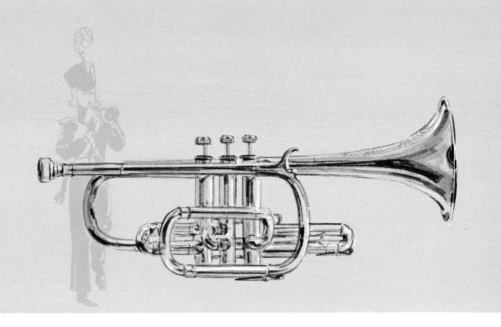

The Cornet

The above picture shows a *cornet*. The parts are the same as for a trumpet. Straightened out, *trumpet and cornet tubes are the same length,* although they can be curved around in slightly different ways. The valves work the same way, and as a matter of fact, it is often difficult to tell the trumpet from the cornet, either by sight or by sound.

An expertly-trained and experienced listener can hear a difference. Expert players will try hard, too, to make a difference between the two instruments, especially if they are being used in the same band. Trumpets usually play with boldness and brilliance. They wake everyone up. The cornetist tries to play with a sweet, mellow sound. He will perhaps use a deep mouthpiece and blow his breath out slowly to make the tones sound smooth. Often he wavers the tone up and down a little by moving his right hand back and forth slightly. This is what we call *vibrato*. It makes the tone warm and velvety, like a beautiful voice.

Some composers think of this voice-like sound that is not as exciting as the true trumpet tone, when they write parts especially for the cornet.

19

The cornet first became popular in France. There it is called *Cornet-a-Pistons,* because the valves work up and down, like the pistons in an automobile motor.

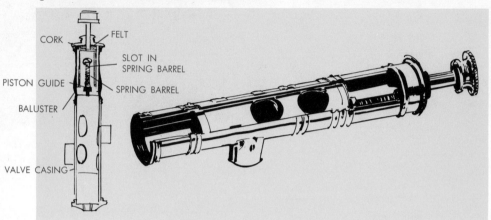

CORK

FELT

SLOT IN
SPRING BARREL

PISTON GUIDE

SPRING BARREL

BALUSTER

VALVE CASING

In America, cornets are seen mostly in school bands. The students like them because they are wound shorter than trumpets. For this reason they are easier to hold and to balance, especially for a beginner between grades four and eight. And of course, students like the cornet when they find out it usually gets to play the melody.

Band directors like the cornet because beginners can more quickly get a smooth, "easy-to-listen-to" tone on it. Girls, especially, find the cornet easier to play than the trumpet.

Parents like cornets, too, because they are one of the less expensive instruments. Also, the tone does not blow the walls of the room down when Johnny and Jane do their practicing in the house every morning.

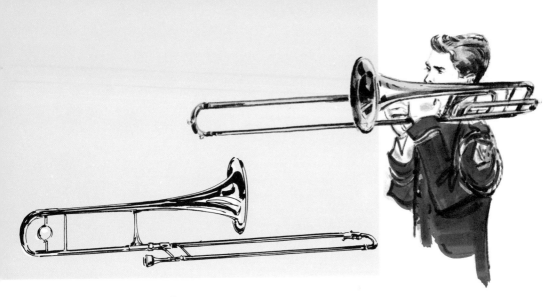

The Trombone

When the band comes down the street, or down the football field, which instruments lead the way? You are right, they are the *slide trombones*. If not 76 of them, there are, we hope, at least six. Why are they in front? If you guessed it is so their slides will not bump into anything — you are right.

And because everyone sees and hears them first, composers of the best street marches write special parts for the trombone called *counter-melodies.* A counter-melody is a melody in the bass which goes with the notes of the main melody being played by the higher sounding instruments, such as the cornets and trumpets. A master at writing marches with many melodies going on at once was John Philip Sousa. He was a former bandmaster of the President of the United States' own band, the Official Marine Corps Band in Washington, D. C.

The name *trombone* is an Italian word that means *big trumpet.*

The tube is twice as long as the trumpet or cornet, or about eight feet. It is very helpful to remember this fact about musical instruments: If you make a tube or string twice as long, you change all the notes a whole octave.

So the trombone, without the slide, plays the same "bugle call notes" as the trumpet, but they all sound eight notes lower.

There are really three different kinds of trombones. In America we see mostly slide trombones. The slide was invented way back around 1300 in northern Italy. It is easy to work in and out. For this reason, the trombone first became known as the *Sackbut,* after a French word *Saqueboute,* meaning to push and pull. Even today in jazz bands all over the world, musicians jokingly call it "the slip horn" or "the old slush pump".

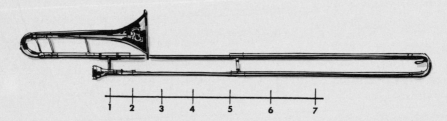

The easiest thing to play on the slide trombone is a chromatic scale going downward. For every three inches you let the slide fall out, any of the bugle call notes is lowered a half-step of the scale. When the slide is closed it is said to be in *first position.* All the way out is *seventh position.* Boys have to wait until their arm has grown to its full length before they can reach that far. There are six stops in between, but there is no mark on the slide to tell you where to stop. Only a good ear for music can help you.

22

TROMBONE POSITIONS

Valve trombones are even more like trumpets. Trumpeters find it easy to play them even though the mouthpiece is bigger. Everything just comes out an octave lower. A valve trombone could be considered a bass trumpet. Some trumpeters can easily switch back and forth between the two instruments. In musicians' language, this is called "doubling".

Here is something odd. Valve trombones today are more popular in Italy than the slide type is, but it was in Italy that the slide was first adapted to the trombones about 700 years ago.

The trombone is capable of playing many different sounding solos. It can play song-like melodies up very high. It can also play heroic march tunes in the powerful low register in a way that is different from any of the other shining brass.

The *bass trombone* is like a fat, overgrown trombone. Besides being bigger and wider, at the back end of the bell it has an extra coil of tubing that fits into the bend. You have to look closely to notice it. The player pushes a valve with his left thumb to allow the air to go through this extra tubing. Then the sound comes out four notes lower. The tone of the bass trombone is big and powerful. Trombonists like to play it because it gives the brass section of the band or orchestra a big healthy "down-in-the-basement" sound.

Trombones were once made in four different sizes. They were given the same names as the four different ranges of people's voices —*soprano, alto, tenor,* and *bass.* The soprano trombone was like a trumpet with a slide on it, or a "half-size trombone." It looked more like a salesman's sample than a real instrument. It was very hard to play. So was the alto trombone. These instruments lost their places to others that could do the job better.

The tenor and bass trombones survived the competition. It is the *tenor trombone* that we see and hear most of the time.

French Horn

There is a funny story about how the *French horn* was invented. Many years ago a stern old musician told his son, "If you don't practice that thing, I'll wrap it around your neck". So he did. And they've wound long brass tubes in a circle ever since.

Of course, we know that this is not really the way the French horn was invented, but it does give us something to smile about. Actually, the circle was big enough for the horn to be slung over the shoulder. That's the way it was held, and with only one hand, too, while the player rode on horseback.

Trumpets were used by the army and by men stationed in watch towers. The French horn was first used by hunters. Hunting calls were really signals to tell friends which way the fox had gone. Horn calls like these could be heard for miles out in the forest.

(Bold and Gay)

A - Hunting we will go.

French horns and trumpets have always had many similarities.

1. Both instruments show man's ability to improve on nature. The first "horn" was made only of a short animal's horn.

2. Both were once simply long wound-up tubes. Today, both have three valves, although the French horn often has extra ones.

3. In the orchestra, both often play similar parts, like fanfares, or long beautiful chords.

4. In addition, both instruments play many solo melodies.

Here are some other comparisons that help you understand more about the French horn.

Mouthpiece. Horn and trumpet mouthpieces are about the same size across. The horn mouthpiece is deeper and is shaped more like a funnel than a cup. This helps the player get low notes. It also helps to make the tone of the horn less brilliant and fiery than the trumpet.

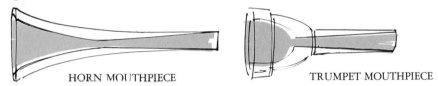

HORN MOUTHPIECE   TRUMPET MOUTHPIECE

Tube. The horn tube, like that of the trumpet, is narrow. This helps it make high notes — almost as high as the trumpet's. But the tube is more than twice as long. So that means it can go way down low, lower than the trombone. It can even play some notes that the tuba does.

AS WRITTEN   NOTES POSSIBLE ON HORN IN F WITHOUT ANY VALVES
1   2   3   4   5   6   7   8   9   10 11 12 13 14 15 16

After valves were invented they were put on horns, too. All the "in between" notes, not written above, became easy to play. And many of the notes pictured here were possible to sound more correctly.

It is interesting to notice some ways in which horns are different from their brass brothers. The way the horn is wound and held causes it to be the only member of the brass instrument family that is played with the bell pointed backwards. This makes its tone sound big, round, and more mysterious than the bold "bell-in-your-face" bright brasses.

A long time ago, players found that the French horn rested easily on their right knee, near their right hand. By putting the hand up into the bell they could do three different tricks.

1. Make the tone softer.

2. Make the pitch go sharper or flatter (a little higher or lower).

3. Make the tone move up a half-step in the scale.

These right hand changes are a part of horn playing even today.

The horn is the only one of the brasses that is fingered with the left hand. Also most horns use *rotary valves.* Notice how they are different from trumpet and cornet piston valves.

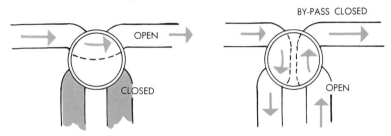

Men who liked to make instruments and invent improvements on them in their workshops soon perfected two different kinds of valves. The piston type, as we said, goes up and down. It is used on most of the instruments of the shining brass family, even on some of the French horns. Horn players in France and England seem to prefer piston valves.

For about the last 100 years, the Germans seem to have led the field in manufacturing "French horns". They equip them with rotary valves. The keys are really levers. When pushed down, they spin a cylinder with slots in it. In an instant, the air is steered from one tube to the other. Rotary valves work a little faster than pistons, and seem to change the notes less noticeably. In Germany, musicians prefer rotary valves on all the other brass instruments, too. In France, they prefer pistons. In America, we use French style trumpets with pistons, and German style horns with rotary valves.

The horn has such a beautiful tone that composers like to write very important solos for it. Some of them are hard to play. The notes go up high, and sometimes they go by very fast. Many horn players have found that their job is made easier by using a horn in B♭. The tube of the B♭ horn is about four feet shorter in length than the F horn. A B♭ French horn is, then, the same length as the trombone, but the tubing is much narrower and the bell is bigger.

To save the players the problem of shifting back and forth between a horn in F and a horn in B♭, clever instrument makers figured out a way to make a *double horn* — two horns in one. It has one mouth-pipe, one bell, one set of valves — but two sets of tubes coming out from the valves, one on each side. The longer ones are for the horn in F, and the shorter ones for the B♭ horn. A fourth valve, one that is pushed with the left hand thumb, changes the instrument from one key to the other. This double horn is used by most of the better players in big bands and orchestras. It gives the player more than one way to solve some difficult playing problems.

The double horn especially, can go both way up high and way down low. It has the widest playing range of any single brass instrument — over three octaves. Only trumpets can go higher. Only tubas can go lower.

French horns are the most beautiful and interesting of the instruments that are "in the middle range". Most big bands and orchestras use four of them to make a quartet. The quartet often plays beautiful chords, as smooth and velvet-like as a church organ.

The horn is not exactly an easy instrument. To be successful with it, a person should have a keen ear for music, a small and strong mouth, and a genuine desire to become an expert player.

In the hands of a serious and well-trained performer, the horn makes probably the most noble and heroic tone of any of the brass instruments. For that reason, sooner or later, every member of the band or orchestra wishes he could play one, too.

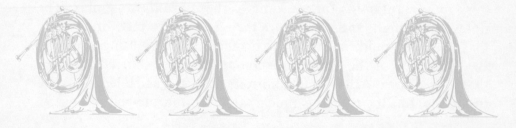

French Horn Substitutes

Remember two of the things we mentioned about the French horn? First, it is not an easy instrument to learn in a hurry. Second, it plays "middle notes", or as we say about voices, notes in the *alto* range.

Most instrumental music lessons in school are given in groups. It is more fun for everyone if progress is made on all the different instruments at about an equal rate of speed. So an easier instrument that is like a French horn has been developed. It is called the *mellophone*. It is easier to play because its tube is a little less than half as long as the French horn's. It fingers exactly the same as a cornet, and uses a mouthpiece just a little bit bigger.

Although the cornet is the most popular brass instrument on which to start, after a few years at least half of the beginners transfer to the alto or bass instruments of the brass family. The "brass team" must have balance of strength in all the positions. There must be equally good players all the way from the top to the bottom of the scale.

Cornet players quickly and easily transfer to any of the other brass instruments, because all the valve instruments work so much alike. Most of the time, a player who changes instruments sticks with his new choice. However, sometimes on TV, we see professionals who can change between mellophone and cornet right during the playing of a single number.

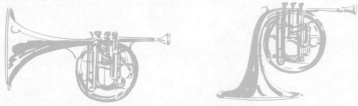

A mellophone can be made with the bell pointed either back or forward. What is the difference? One is much easier to hear than the other. One has the bell pointed in the same direction as all the other shining brass. It is correct to think that brass instruments are something like rifles — they send the sound the fastest in the direction in which they are aimed.

The other French horn substitutes are called *alto horns.* They should be thought of not as big trumpets, but as big cornets. Their tube is a little broader, and so is their tone. The tube is about two feet longer than a cornet, so even though it fingers the same, every note comes out five notes lower.

Alto horns are made "bell up" or "bell front".

Alto horns were developed and perfected by a very famous French instrument maker named Antoine Joseph Sax. Can you guess what other family of instruments he also invented?

Bass Brass

Did you ever think it would be fun to work in a candy factory? How about a pretzel factory? Think about it a minute. You could cut the strips of dough in different lengths. Experiment, use your imagination, wrap the dough into different shapes, and twist it up into all kinds of forms and sizes.

Then you could try for a job in a brass instrument factory. Maybe they would have you doing almost the same thing. Look closely in this chapter and see all the different ways that big, shining brass instruments have been shaped.

Many of the instruments have been designed with the idea that they would be used on the march. The Army and Navy bands have always had a big influence on brass instrument design.

During the Civil War, one bandmaster designed a group of instruments all of which pointed back over the shoulder, so that the troops following the band could better hear the music and the march beat. This idea did not last long, however.

The big basses are heavy and hard to carry. If wound in a big circle, they can rest on the player's shoulder. An old army tuba with the bell turned sideways, is called a *helicon*. It looks like a giant French horn turned upside down. It was easy to carry on the march.

The famous bandmaster, John Philip Sousa, liked the idea of the big coil that would allow the instrument to rest on a man's shoulder, but he wanted the bell twisted around so it faced front, and toward the audience. Such a tuba is now called a *Sousaphone*. It is this instrument that we see most often in present day school bands.

These tubas are said to be in "double B♭", or BB♭. This means that they play *two octaves* below the cornets. It also means that the pipe is not merely twice as long, but four times as long! Tubas play the lowest notes of any of the family of shining brass instruments.

Tubas play the bass line, the same as the left hand does in piano music. When we listen to music, our ears first hear the top notes, or the melody. Next, they catch the notes that are on the bottom, the bass. Composers never forget this. They are always careful to write interesting parts for the bass instruments. Tuba parts are always great fun, and, of course, are very important in making a good sounding group. Bandmasters have a slogan like this: "Good tubas — good band".

In symphony and opera orchestras the *upright bass* is used. The sound goes straight up and bounces off the ceiling. This makes the tone sound softer, and as if it comes from the distance. That's the same way it is with the French horn, too, because the bell is not

34

aimed directly at the listener's ear. Musicians think up funny names for almost all of the instruments. They jokingly call upright model brasses "raincatchers".

The same kind of big tuba, but with the bell twisted to the front is called a *recording model*. Back in the days after the first world war when big bands and orchestras first made records, it was hard to get the tuba to sound the way a tuba should. Remember, all this was long before Hi-Fi, Stereo, or TV. In laboratory tests, engineers and music conductors decided that the tuba with the bell front sounded the best on the records. It blended in best with the trombones and with the trumpets to give a smooth balance of sound.

Concert tubas are not held over the shoulder, but are balanced on the edge of the chair or in the player's lap. The big bells are made removable so they not only can be turned in any direction, but can also be taken off to allow the instrument to be packed and carried more easily.

Yes, tubas come in different lengths, as well as in different shapes. In orchestras, the men use either the big tubas in double C—CC,—or smaller ones in F. In bands, the most popular tuba is the one in BB♭, but the smaller E♭ tuba is also very useful. It is shorter, lighter in weight, can use a slightly smaller mouthpiece, and is a little easier to play, especially for young beginners.

Contrary to popular opinion, it does not take lots and lots of wind to make the tuba work. It is not a matter of making like the old wolf did to the three little pigs when he said, "I'll huff and I'll puff, and I'LL BLOW YOUR HOUSE DOWN" (like I puff on my tuba). As with any other brass instrument, it only takes enough breath to buzz the lips, and then to keep that vibration going.

Tuba players usually are selected from those who naturally have a large mouth formation. Large lips fit most comfortably into a large-size mouthpiece. The tuba mouthpiece is quite wide and quite deep. It has to be, to get a sixteen-foot long tube into vibration.

35

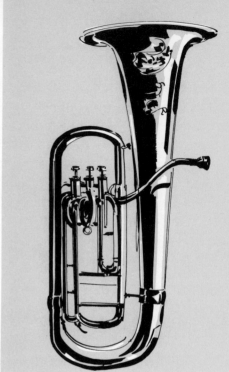

The Baritone Horn

In England, they like them *upright*.

In Germany, the *oval* shape is very popular.

In America we prefer our baritone horns to look like a small, halfsize, *bell-front* tuba.

You hold these instruments against your chest, like you would carry home a big bag of groceries.

The *Baritone Horn* is half tuba, half cornet. It is also half-way in-between in size, since it is half as long as a tuba, but twice as long as a cornet. *All three instruments finger the same.* Three players, pressing down the same valves on the three different instruments, could easily play the same melody together perfectly. Each instrument would sound one octave apart from the other. What they would play would look like this if written on the *grand staff.*

Trumpets read this

Baritones and trombones read top notes, tubas, the bottom notes

Baritone horns are used only in bands. They do the same job that cellos do in an orchestra. Sometimes they play the bass part. Sometimes they play the same melody that the cornets and trumpets are sounding up higher. Very often they take turns with the trombones playing *counter-melodies.* Do you remember what a counter-melody is from our discussion of the trombone?

The baritone is so similar to the cornet that very often cornet players transfer to it in order to help make a better band. Also, to make this transfer even easier for the players, most band music has baritone horn parts that are written in the treble clef, or G-Clef. The player reads the same as for cornet music, but the notes come out an octave lower.

Really, then, the baritone is a *bass clef,* or *F-clef* instrument. While wider, it is exactly the same length as its close cousins, the valve trombone and the slide trombone. Because the instruments have the same range, use the same mouthpiece, and can read from the same F-clef music, many students in school bands learn both the baritone horn and the tenor trombone, and trade off between them, either for fun or to help the band.

37

Comparisons

We have described many different instruments from the *Shining Brass* family. All of them are similar, yet each is a little different. This chart shows how these instruments would compare in size if their tubing were straightened out.

The trumpet and cornet are the same length. The bell of the cornet is a little larger and wider.

The alto horn's tube is larger than the cornet's. Note that the bell of the mellophone is larger than the alto horn's.

The French horn in F is almost twice as long as the mellophone.

The tube of the French horn in B♭ is the same length as that of the trombone.

The shape of the trombone tube is like that of the trumpet, but it is twice as long.

The shape of the baritone horn tube is similar to that of the cornet (large and wide bell). Baritones and trombones are the same length.

The tuba in E♭ is twice as long as the mellophone and, like it, the bell is large and wide.

The tuba or sousaphone in BB♭ is twice as long as the baritone, and four times as long as the trumpet.

The three valve *Shining Brass* are played alike.

38

TRUMPET IN B♭   CORNET IN B♭   ALTO HORN IN E♭   MELLOPHONE IN E♭   FRENCH HORN IN F

39

FRENCH HORN IN B♭   TROMBONE IN B♭   BARITONE HORN IN B♭   BASS TUBA IN E♭   TUBA OR SOUSAPHONE IN BB♭

ABOUT THE AUTHOR

Daniel B. Tetzlaff has devoted his life to music and has an impressive background. In 1946 he graduated from the University of Minnesota with distinction in Music Education. For seven years he played the trumpet with the Minneapolis Symphony Orchestra under such distinguished conductors as Mitropolous, Dorati, Stokowski, Kostelanetz and Ormandy, and for six consecutive years he was elected to the trumpet section of the *American Bandmasters Band* by officials of the National Band Clinic. He has been an outstanding conductor himself, and has taught at several universities and colleges of music. Mr. Tetzlaff is also a guest lecturer and writes for many music journals. At the present time, he holds a position with the Music Department of the Minneapolis Public Schools.